Gyo Obata

by Eric Kudalis

Capstone Press
MINNEAPOLIS

Printed in the United States of America.

Capstone Press • 2440 Fernbrook Lane • Minneapolis, MN 55447

Editorial Director   John Coughlan
Managing Editor   Tom Streissguth
Production Editor   James Stapleton
Book Design   Tim Halldin

Library of Congress Cataloging-in-Publication Data

Kudalis, Eric, 1960--
    Gyo Obata / Eric Kudalis
      p. cm. -- (Architects--artists who build)
    Includes bibliographical references and index.
    Summary: Profiles the life and career of the San Francisco-born architect, strongly affected by his Japanese heritage, who has designed hundreds of buildings all over the world.
    ISBN 1-56065-311-6
    1. Obata, Gyo, 1923- --Themes, motives--Juvenile literature. 2. Architecture, Modern--20th century--United States--Juvenile literature. [1. Obata, Gyo, 1923- . 2. Architects. 3. Architecture, Modern--20th century.] I. Title. II. Series.
NA737.O2K8 1996
    720'.92--dc20   95-435
    [B]   CIP
                                               AC

Table of Contents

Chapter 1

Sea Shells and Sunshine

A giant glass seashell rises along the shores of the Gulf of Mexico. Colorful walls support the shell. Below, birds swoop between the branches of tropical plants. Visitors stroll through a Forested Wetlands exhibit.

This is the Florida **Aquarium** in Tampa. The aquarium's exhibits tell the story of Florida's water habitats. Visitors learn about wetlands, beaches, coral reefs, and the sea. The

A roof of glass and steel soars over the Florida Aquarium.

The columns and walls of King Saud University in Saudi Arabia reflect the colors of the desert.

exhibits feature more than 4,300 native plants and animals.

Gyo Obata, an architect who lives in St. Louis, Missouri, designed the Florida Aquarium. He has designed hundreds of buildings all over the world. As the co-chairman for Hellmuth Obata & Kassabaum

(HOK), he also leads one of the largest architecture firms in the world.

The Obata Method

Obata says that his buildings are designed from the inside out. First, he sits down with the client to learn what the client needs. He wants to know what must go inside a building before he decides on the outside.

The glass roof at the Florida Aquarium lets the bright sunshine of the region into the building.

For the Florida project, he learned that the aquarium needed two large exhibits designed around a public **lobby**. The aquarium also needed a gift shop, a cafeteria, offices, classrooms, and a children's exhibit area.

Obata toured the site. Tampa and its sister city, St. Petersburg, enjoy warm, tropical winds from the Gulf of Mexico. This tropical climate, and Florida's seashore and sunshine, inspired his design.

He began by making sketches and drawings. Then he built three-dimensional **models** from his sketches. The models helped him decide how the sunshine would flow into the building. Obata believes that light, sun, and outside views are important parts of any well-designed building. The models also show how people will walk through a building, and how cars will approach it.

Obata designed the aquarium's glass roof in the shape of a seashell. He chose several bright colors for the outside walls. These colors express the site's warm climate.

Obata and his team of architects entered the sketches into a computer. The computers helped them work out the final design.

Today, adults and children walk through the Florida Aquarium. Sharks and alligators snap their sharp teeth, as octopuses and dolphins swim about. Herons step carefully through the wetlands. With Obata's designs, Florida's water environments come to life.

Chapter 2

Learning about Architecture

Ever since Gyo Obata was six years old, he wanted to be an architect.

He was born in San Francisco, California, in 1923 and grew up in nearby Berkeley. His father, Chiura Obata, was a famous artist who taught at the University of California at Berkeley. He had moved to San Francisco from Japan around 1900.

Chiura Obata brought sumi-e, a Japanese ink-and-brush painting style, to the United States. Gyo's mother, Haruko Obata, was also an artist. She was well known for the art of ikebana (Japanese flower arranging). Both parents inspired Gyo. They also taught him the importance of listening carefully.

Learning in Japan

When he was six years old, Gyo spent a year at his grandmother's house in Japan. There he learned about Japanese architecture. This building style closely imitates the forms of nature.

Obata fondly recalls his grandmother's house. Throughout the house were shoji screens and tatami mats. Shoji screens are made of rice paper on wooden frames. Tatami mats, woven of rice straw, are used for sitting when eating. In the back of the house was a guest room that opened to a garden. Its simple design made the house feel peaceful and private.

Obata entered the architecture school at the University of California in 1941, but he soon had to leave. On December 7, 1941, the Japanese army bombed Pearl Harbor, the U.S.

naval base in Hawaii. Suddenly, the United States was at war with Japan.

Nearly 100,000 Japanese lived on the West Coast of the United States at the beginning of World War II. Many people disliked the Japanese-Americans. The bombing of Pearl Harbor made the situation even worse.

The U. S. government soon decided to move the Japanese-Americans to **internment camps**. Many Japanese-Americans lost their homes, businesses, and property.

The government notified Obata and his family that they must move to a camp in Utah.

This internment camp in Topaz, Utah—and many others in the western United States—held Japanese families during World War II.

Obata's father urged Gyo to leave the West Coast.

Gyo applied to several universities throughout the country. Many schools would not accept him because he was a Japanese-American. Finally, Washington University in St. Louis accepted him. The night before his family moved to the camp, Gyo left for St. Louis.

A Different Place

Obata saw that in the Midwest most people didn't hate the Japanese. They lived far from the West Coast, and they didn't worry about air attacks from Japan.

In St. Louis, Obata concentrated on his school work. After graduating from Washington University in 1945, he studied at Cranbrook Academy of Art in Michigan. There he received a master's degree in architecture and urban design in 1946. Soon he began his architectural career.

Gyo Obata's firm designed this planetarium at the St. Louis Science Center.

Chapter 3
Building a Career

Obata is a trim man with graying hair and glasses. He jogs or rides his bike every day for exercise. He has the energy of someone much younger, and he always keeps his office busy.

Hellmuth Obata & Kassabaum has offices in 12 U.S. cities and six foreign cities. More than 1,400 people work for the company, including 300 at the home office in St. Louis.

HOK's main office is on the sixth floor of Metropolitan Square, a 42-story office building in downtown St. Louis. Obata designed the

801 Grand is the address, and the name, of this office tower in Des Moines, Iowa.

Obata studied the natural shapes of seashells while working on these plans for a new building.

building in 1989. Marble, granite, and brass decorate the lobby. Large **murals** on the walls show the history of St. Louis.

The offices of HOK are quite different from the lobby. Elevator doors open to a bright white reception hall. The office is very simple and

neat. It looks much like the simple style of traditional Japanese architecture.

Architects work just beyond the reception area. **Drafting boards** and computer terminals are their basic design tools. Sketches and computer drawings line the walls.

Obata's own office is filled with books and architectural drawings. A window overlooks downtown St. Louis. Near his desk is a picture of his mother wearing a traditional Japanese kimono.

After finishing college, Obata became successful quickly. He worked hard and studied the work of many great architects. At Cranbrook Academy of Art, he studied under the famous Finnish architect Eliel Saarinen. Saarinen taught him the importance of combining different elements into a single project.

Obata also admired the famous architect Frank Lloyd Wright, who is known for his many houses in the **Prairie Style**. Other influences on Obata's style were Mies van der Rohe and Walter Gropius. Both of these German architects moved to the United States in the 1930s.

Learning on the Job

After college, Obata worked in the busy Chicago offices of Skidmore Owings and Merrill (SOM). At an early age, he learned how a large firm operated. He saw that architects, engineers, and other professionals worked closely together to design a building.

Obata soon moved back to St. Louis, where he worked with the famous Japanese-American architect Minoru Yamasaki. He helped design the Lambert-St. Louis International Airport.

In 1955, Obata joined George Hellmuth and George E. Kassabaum to form HOK. The three men wanted their firm to grow, and they made big plans right from the start. After Hellmuth retired in 1978, and Kassabaum died in 1982, Obata continued to push the firm in new directions. HOK designed churches, schools, hospitals, airports, high-rises, zoos, shopping centers, and many other kinds of projects.

Chapter 4

How Obata Designs

Many architects have a distinct style. Frank Lloyd Wright's work is horizontal and uses a lot of wood and brick. Frank Gehry, an architect in Los Angeles, often uses odd shapes and forms. Gyo Obata avoids a particular style. As a result, each of his buildings looks different.

Thinking about the Site

When Obata is working on a new project, he travels to the site and observes the nearby

A quiet stream flows past the entrance to the St. Louis Zoo.

The final designs for the Florida Aquarium include this view of the floor plan.

buildings. He wants his buildings to fit with their neighbors, and to blend with their natural settings. He also observes the sunlight. Obata wants his buildings to have plenty of natural daylight. For the Florida Aquarium, he chose bright colors because the sun is bright in Florida. The colors also make the building look fun–because visiting an aquarium should be fun.

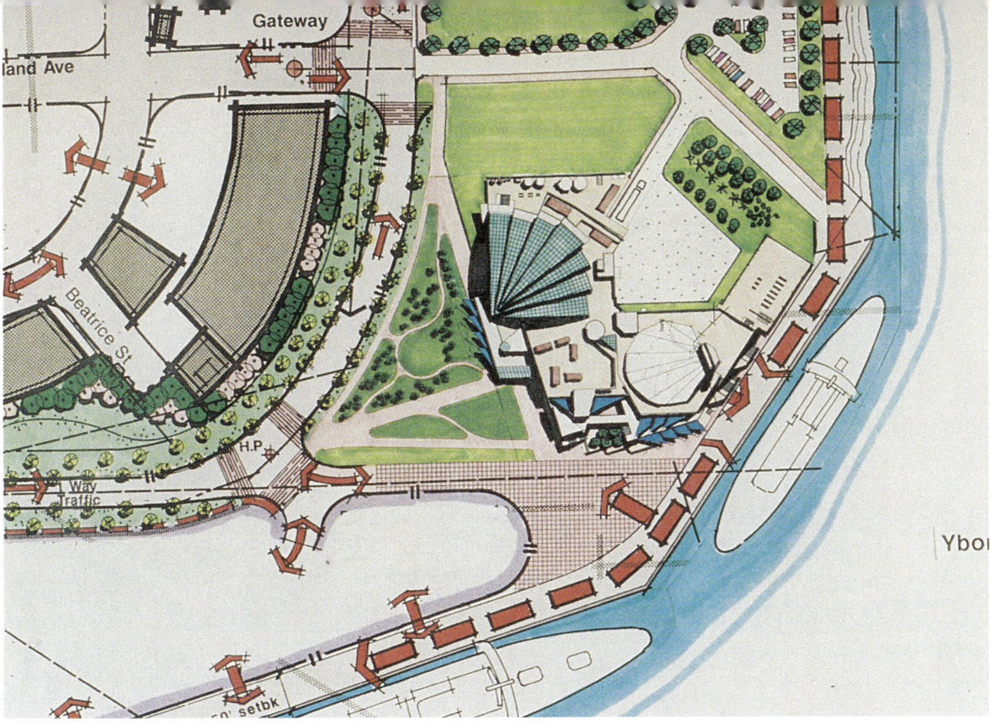

The aquarium lies at the edge of the Gulf of Mexico.

For the Oriole Park at Camden Yards, built in Baltimore, Maryland, Obata's firm designed an open-air baseball stadium with a brick exterior. They chose red brick because

A final drawing shows the aquarium and its surroundings.

Baltimore has many historic red-brick buildings.

In 1984, Obata designed King Saud University in Saudi Arabia. To shield people from the hot desert sun, he included shaded walkways and small windows. Sand-colored **concrete** walls reflect the desert sands.

In Battle Creek, Michigan, Obata designed the corporate headquarters of the Kellogg Company, the cereal maker. The company believes in protecting the land. Obata chose red brick, yellow limestone, **terra cotta**, pale-green glass, and **teakwood**–all materials that reflect natural colors.

In 1983, Obata designed an ice-skating rink for the Galleria in Dallas, Texas. The Galleria combines shopping, entertainment, offices, and a hotel. He used many polished surfaces to create a glittering surface.

All these buildings are different from each other, because the clients–and the sites–are all different.

A tall, spiraling steeple rises above this new Mormon temple in Independence, Missouri.

Chapter 5

A Tour of Gyo Obata's Works

Here are some of Gyo Obata's best-known projects.

The National Air and Space Museum Washington, D.C.

Airplanes swoop down from the ceiling, as if suspended in flight. A huge missile rises in the main lobby. The Apollo spacecraft, which once stood on the moon, now rests on the museum's floor.

Historic planes crowd the airspace at the National Air and Space Museum.

The National Air and Space Museum, on the Capitol Mall, is one of the most popular museums in Washington, D.C. About 10 million visitors wander through its galleries each year. More than 65 aircraft and 100 spacecraft display achievements in flight.

For the project, Obata designed four sections clad in marble. Three glass-enclosed exhibit bays connect the sections. The 630,000-square-foot museum has a library, offices, two theaters, and an auditorium. The museum also has a domed **planetarium** that shows dazzling films of flight.

The Living World/St. Louis Zoo
St. Louis, Missouri

The natural world is featured at St. Louis's newest zoo addition, finished in 1989. Through educational exhibits and displays, children and

Multimedia exhibits surround visitors to The Living World museum at the St. Louis Zoo.

adults learn about wildlife preservation and environmental conservation.

Two exhibit halls combine high-technology displays with living animals. A stream from the Missouri Ozarks flows through the Hall of Ecology. Hands-on exhibits teach about the world's many environments. In the Hall of Animals, an image of Charles Darwin greets museum visitors. Darwin was a scientist who studied evolution. According to evolutionary

The architect allowed space for large, three-dimensional exhibits.

Small sculptures, such as this bronze frog, catch the eye at The Living World.

theories, simple organisms and animals develop into more complex organisms and animals as time passes.

The two exhibit halls contain 85 three-minute films, 30 computer stations, 50 video screens, and a dozen interactive videos. More than 150 animals also fill the exhibits.

Oriole Park at Camden Yards
Camden Yards Twin-Stadium Complex
Baltimore, Maryland
Wooden baseball bats smack baseballs, sending cracking echoes through the park. The bright sun shines down as the wind whistles

across the field. Vendors walk up and down the aisles selling hot dogs and peanuts.

Built in 1992 as the new home of the Baltimore Orioles, this 46,000-seat stadium is an old-fashioned baseball park. The brick exterior matches the brick buildings in the

neighborhood. Unlike many domed stadiums, Camden Yards feels like part of the city.

HOK has designed many sports facilities. They also designed Joe Robbie Stadium in Florida for the Miami Dolphins, Jacobs Field for the Cleveland Indians, and Coors Field in Denver for the Colorado Rockies.

King Khalid International Airport Riyadh, Saudi Arabia

Obata and his firm have designed many projects in foreign countries. This airport was built in Saudi Arabia, the home of important Islamic shrines, in 1983. The airport is unusual because it contains a **mosque** (an Islamic house of prayer). Before designing the mosque, Obata spoke to an expert in traditional Islamic architecture.

Each airplane terminal is designed around **pavilions** that surround garden courts. The mosque is shaped like a hexagon. It has six 170-foot (52-meter) sides and a domed roof.

Two rows of flags line the entranceway to King Khalid Airport in Saudi Arabia.

Because the airport serves as a gateway to the country, the architect believed it was important to use traditional Islamic forms.

Geometric forms such as the triangle are common in Islamic art. Obata used these forms throughout the King Khalid Airport.

Throughout the airport, Obata uses triangular forms. Within the airport, he also placed many gardens and fountains. These are also common details in Islamic artworks.

St. Louis Union Station
St. Louis, Missouri

The whistles of arriving trains are silent. Shoppers mingle where trains once chugged along the platforms.

This renewed train station is located in downtown St. Louis. The station was originally built in 1894. By the 1970s, it was empty and quiet.

Today the restored 825,000-square-foot station contains retail stores, restaurants, and a 550-room hotel. The market also has a landscaped park, lake, and beer garden.

The station's 230-foot (70-meter) clock tower has become a St. Louis landmark. One of the most beautiful spaces is the grand hall. Here the architects restored a barrel-vaulted ceiling. The ceiling glows with gold leaf and stained glass.

Chapter 6
Future Architecture

Gyo Obata believes that architects should be generalists. That means an architect needs to be an artist, a mathematician, a technical expert, and a humanist.

An architect also has to understand all the mechanical systems that go into a building. Lighting, heating, ventilation, and electronics are all part of big buildings. There are elevators, fire alarms, electronic doors, and computers. Architects need to know how all these systems work within a building.

The Galleria project in Dallas includes an indoor skating rink.

A city hospital, for instance, must have life-saving equipment. An architect has to know how to design space for X-ray machines, radiation machines, and operating rooms.

An architect also designs buildings to be comfortable. Many people are in hospitals because they are sick. But many hospitals are cold and frightening places. A good architect designs a hospital that creates a soothing environment for patients. By adding lots of windows, natural light, and warm colors, an architect can create a comforting hospital.

Obata believes that future architects will face many challenges. One of the most difficult will be the growing population. Humans are using up natural resources, such as wood from forests and fuels from the earth. Future architects need to be more concerned about the environment. This will make sustainable architecture important in the future.

Sustain means to support or maintain. Sustainable architecture, then, maintains the environment. A sustainable building conserves energy and uses resources carefully. It uses

only wood taken from forests that will be replanted for future generations. Also, a building's exhaust system should only emit non-toxic fumes that won't kill animals, birds, or plants.

A Global Architecture

In addition to learning about the environment, a successful future architect must learn about other cultures. Obata says we live in a global economy, and foreign projects will become more important to future architects.

Countries in Eastern Europe and Asia are growing rapidly. Places like Poland, eastern Germany, and China are changing fast. They are welcoming new ideas and new projects. Architects of the future will have many chances to build there. Learning a foreign language will help them understand these cultures.

The Architect's Goal

Architecture is a creative profession. For Obata, the joy of being an architect is working with people. Every building is designed for people, and a well-designed building will make their lives more pleasant. If a building is well ventilated, has plenty of light, is easy to work and live in, and is beautiful, then people are happy.

Glossary

aquarium–a place for the exhibition of water animals and plants

cement–a material made of special, powdered rock and clay. These ingredients form a paste with water and dry to a solid mass.

column–a vertical support, such as a post

drafting board–a high desk on which architects and engineers design buildings

internment camps–places where people are confined against their will

lobby–an open, public area on the ground floor of a building

models–small, three-dimensional copies of a building or project

mosque–an Islamic house of prayer and worship

mural–a large painting done on a wall or ceiling

pavilion–a large tent or structure that is supported by columns instead of walls

planetarium–an auditorium in which a projector shows images of the sky and space

Prairie Style–an architectural style that uses mostly horizontal lines and a lot of wood trim

teakwood–wood from a tall confier (evergreen) tree of southeastern Asia

terra cotta–a hard clay that can be molded and painted for decoration on buildings.

Some Useful Addresses

AIA (American Institute of Architects) Careers Program
1735 New York Avenue
Washington, DC   20006

National Institute for Architectural Education
30 W. 22nd St.
New York, NY   10010

To Learn More

Anger, David. *Cesar Pelli.* Minneapolis: Capstone Press, 1996.

_____. *Robert A. M. Stern.* Minneapolis: Capstone Press, 1996.

Horwitz, Elinor Lander. *How to Wreck a Building.* New York: Pantheon, 1992.

Kudalis, Eric. *Michael Graves.* Minneapolis: Capstone Press, 1996.

Lewis, Alun. *SuperStructures.* New York: Viking Press, 1979.

Photo credits: Robert Azzi: pp. 6, 37; George Cott: pp. 22, 33; Nancy Moriguchi, Japanese-American National Museum: p. 13; John Rubin: p. 10; Balthazar Korab: pp. 4, 7, 8, 27, 43; Gregory Murphey: p. 38; Robert Pettus: pp. 15, 31, 32; George Silk: pp. 28, 30; Jeff Goldberg: pp. 34-35; Hellmuth,Obata & Kassabaum: pp. 18-19, 24, 25, 40.

Index